WELCOME

A traditional taste of Wales. Welsh-insp classic Welsh cakes and bara brith to n traditional like Welsh rarebit. Wales is renowned for its traditional recipes and most of these are also suitable for vegetarians.

I was born and raised in Wales and my wife and two sons, Rhys and Owain moved away to England in 2001. My summers were spent on the Welsh Coast in places like Porthcawl, Mumbles, Langland Bay and Caswell Bay. I have fond memories of picking periwinkles with my Nan on Langland Bay and then taking them home to cook and eat with a pin.

My work took me to live in Kent, Edinburgh, and Manchester, and I returned to Wales in 2018 with my wife Nicola. I had forgotten how many things I had missed about the welsh food and welsh psyche. In my opinion, the smell when you walk into Swansea market should be bottled and sold as Eau de Cymru.

A simple step by step recipe book that starts you off on your journey to discovering traditional welsh food.

The recipes are mostly quick, easy, cheap, and delicious. The recipes also contain many easy to find ingredients that are already in your cupboard.

I am not an expert, and certainly not a trained chef – those who know me, know me as someone who simply loves food and loves eating. Hence the recipes being loosely grouped into food types. It is difficult for me to add the servings or number of people the recipes cover, as my appetite is not a good measure of portion size!

I also have not included nutritional values or calorific values, as this is not supposed to be a healthy book – food is to be enjoyed, and I believe in 'everything in moderation'. If you want to eat it – eat it, just make sure you factor healthy food choices and exercise into your daily routine.

Most of the ingredients are as welsh as possible, but please feel free to experiment and explore with your own local versions, and please share them with me.

I have unashamedly named many of the dishes after family members and friends as without them, I would them, I would not be the person I am today, on top of that there is nothing better in life than sharing a meal and a drink with family and friends – unfortunately it has taken the Covid Pandemic to teach us what really matters in life.

Over the past two years, I have been seeking out and rediscovering the traditional welsh recipes and named them after local areas. I hope you enjoy them as much as I do. As a Committee Member of the Wooden Spoon Wales Rugby Charity – proceeds from this book will be donated to the charity.

See the links below and please contact me if you have any projects / developments that you think Wooden Spoon could support you with.

Facebook.com/spoonwales

Twitter.com/SpoonWales

www.woodenspoon.org.uk/region/wales

dai.fussell@hotmail.co.uk

© Dai Fussell 2020

The right of Dai Fussell as author of this work has been asserted by him in accordance with the Copyright, Design and Patents Act 1998. All rights reserved. No part of this publication may be produced, stored, or transmitted in any form or by any means, electronic, photocopying, recording or otherwise without the prior permission of Dai Fussell.

This book is dedicated to my parents Norma and Peter.

CONTENTS

Traditional Welsh (Pages 4 – 14).

1. Welsh Rarebit
2. Le Welsh
3. Welsh Cakes
4. Bara Brith
5. Porthcawl Bisgedi
6. Newton Bakestones
7. Rest Bay Bisgedi
8. Nottage Pottage
9. Jolly Sailor Crempog
10. Coney Beach Onion Cakes
11. Cows Cawl

Family and Friends (Pages 15 – 25)

12. Nannie and Noah's Pasties
13. Norma's Curry
14. Cow Chow
15. Rhys has a Beef with Training
16. Owains Gym Recovery
17. Bethan's Bakes
18. Angharad's Cheesecake
19. Wok 'n' Roll
20. Cow Pie Roll
21. The Morning After – Sian's Salvation
22. The Morning After – Cows Fry Up.

WELSH RAREBIT

How could I possibly start a welsh recipe book without perhaps the best-known welsh (and further afield) favourite? Welsh rabbit (original spelling) is a traditional Welsh dish made with melted cheese and various other ingredients and served hot, after being poured over slices of toasted bread or served in a dish. The names of the dish originate from 18th-century Britain, despite the dish containing no rabbit meat.

4 slices of bread

30g of softened butter

1 teaspoon of English Mustard

¼ teaspoon salt

A light dust of Cayenne pepper

¼ teaspoon Worcestershire Sauce

200g Caerphilly / Cheddar Cheese

2 tablespoons of beer (or milk if you must!)

Cream the butter in a bowl and stir in the other ingredients. Only toast the bread on one side. Take the mixture from the bowl and spread in on the untoasted side of the bread. Put it back under the grill so the mixture melts onto the toast.

LE WELSH

In some parts of France (Lille and French Flanders) Welsh Rarebit it is known as Le Welsh, Un Welsh or Croque Gallois. Use the above ingredients – minus the Cayenne Pepper. Use Dijon mustard instead of English. You will also need two eggs and slices of ham.

Heat the oven to 180 °C. Lay the bread in a baking dish and lay a slice of ham on top of the bread. Melt the cheese in a saucepan until smooth and then add the other ingredients and stir together well. Pour the mixture over the slices of bread / ham and put into the pre-heated oven for 6-8 minutes. Whilst the mixture is in the oven – poach the eggs ready to put on top of the slices when they come out of the oven.

You can add a poached egg on top of the Welsh recipe which is then known as a Buck Rarebit.

WELSH CAKES

These little bad boys are my downfall and perhaps the reason why I have the nickname Cow. It's either because I could eat these 'till the cows come home', but it's probably because I can eat so many that I have four stomachs!

Welsh cakes are a cross between a cookie, a scone, and a pancake but they are truly unlike any of these things when it comes to taste and texture. They are the size of chubby cookie, made from ingredients like a stone, but they are cooked like a pancake on a griddle, they are not baked.

Welsh Cakes are an example of a unique and traditional food that reflects the resourceful, wholesome, and practical nature of the Welsh people. Made from simple pantry items like flour, sugar, milk and butter, Welsh Cakes are considered a special treat since they take a great deal of time and effort to make. Being griddled, they pretty much must be made by hand and therefore there are very few commercial makers of these cakes in the world. Traditionally they were cooked over a hot bakestone, but iron griddles were later used and are now the predominant method used to cook them.

The best place to get them is in Swansea or Cardiff Markets, or the best I have tasted are from Home and Colonial Fine foods in John Street, Porthcawl, where you can see them being griddled in the window.

1lb of Flour

1 teaspoon of baking powder

1 pinch allspice

1 pinch salt

120g butter

110g lard

200g castor sugar

100g seedless raisins

2 eggs (beaten)

Milk

Stir together the allspice, salt, baking powder and flour into a largish bowl. Rub in the lard and the butter. Add the raisins and sugar. Add the beaten eggs to the bowl. Add in enough milk until the dough is fairly stiff. Take the mixture and roll it out onto a lightly floured flat surface. Roll it to a thickness of around 10mm and then use around a 5cm (2 inch) pastry cutter to cut them out into round shapes. Cook on the greased bakestone / griddle for about 3-5 minutes depending on the thickness of the bakestone / griddle. You could also use a thick based frying pan. Sprinkle with castor sugar and serve warm.

BARA BRITH

Bara brith derives its name from the Welsh language, bara meaning bread and brith translating as speckled. It is claimed to have been invented by a Welsh chef who added dried fruit and spices to a bread dough, creating the first version of the traditional Welsh tea loaf. There are lots of different recipes, but the common ingredient is cold tea.

I was lucky enough to spend two weeks on rugby tour In Argentina and found a version of bara brith which was known as torta negra ("black cake"). One of the most traditional foods coming out of Patagonia, (where they speak welsh), it was brought by the Welsh settlers who started arriving in the country in 1865. So, whether it's the Chubut Valley or the Rhondda Valley – everyone loves bara brith.

200g mixed dried fruit

200ml cold tea (no milk)

80g of soft brown sugar

60g butter

Pinch of salt

2 tablespoons of marmalade (ring in version) lemon or orange

340g of self-raising wholemeal flower

1 teaspoon mixed spice

1 large egg

Loaf Tin

Honey to Glaze

Soak the mixed dried fruit in the cold tea for 4 hours. After 4 hours strain the fruit and keep the liquid.

In a mixing bowl stir together the flour, mixed spice, and sugar. Mix in the marmalade, butter, egg, and salt.

Stir in the fruit and add the liquid a bit at a time whilst kneading gently until the dough is an elastic / dropping consistency. Place the dough into the tin and leave in a warm place for two hours.

Put into a pre-heated oven on 160º C for 50- 60 minutes until risen and firm to the touch. Glaze with the honey and allow to cool. Serve sliced – with or without butter depending on your taste.

PORTHCAWL BISGEDI BISCOTTI

Welsh Italians are an ethnic minority of Italian or mixed Italian and Welsh descent living in Wales. Most Italian immigration to Wales took place in the 19th and early 20th centuries, with the largest number of migrants settling in Glamorgan and Newport. This recipe is a mixture of those cultures.

100g butter

40g icing sugar

1 ½ tablespoons of honey

100g of plain flour

75g of finely chopped hazelnuts

Icing sugar for dusting

Cream the butter, sugar, and honey together in a bowl until light and fluffy. Fold in the flour and nuts until it forms a smooth dough. Place in small heaps on greased baking sheets about 3cm apart.

Put into a pre-heated oven on 180°C for about 15 minutes until firm and golden. Cool slightly and dust with icing sugar.

NEWTON BAKESTONE CAKES

These delicious cakes are more like scones than cakes. They were cooked on a bakestone as many homes did not have the luxury of an oven. You can use a griddle of heavy based frying pan.

220g Flour

Pinch of salt

15g baking powder

60g butter

Single cream

Sift the salt, baking powder and flour into a bowl and then rub in the butter till it resembles breadcrumbs. Add enough cream to form a stiff dough. On a floured flat surface, roll the mixture out to around ½ cm and cut into circles around 7cm wide.

Ensure the griddle is lightly greased and cook on both sides until golden brown. Split in half and serve hot with butter.

REST BAY BISGEDI

Rest Bay is one of several beaches stretching from Sker Point through to Ogmore. Porthcawl's promenade, built in 1887 to commemorate Queen Victoria's Golden Jubilee and restored in 1996, runs along the seafront from Lock's Common in the west to the harbour, before joining the eastern promenade and leading to Coney Beach and Griffin Park. There are many cafes, bars, restaurants, and hotels located along the promenade which offer spectacular views across the Bristol Channel on top of serving great local food.

A new state-of-the-art water sports centre overlooks Porthcawl's Blue Flag Rest Bay beach and will provide the perfect base for adventure seekers eager to sample South Wales' outdoor activity offering in 2020. Pack some of these into your bag before you set out on walk along the front.

225g almond paste

2 large egg whites, beaten (plus one extra in case)

130g of icing sugar

250g of crushed almonds

Preheat the oven to 180°C and grease a baking tray.

Crumble the almond paste into a bowl and beat in the egg whites and icing sugar – this can be done by hand or by electric mixer. The mixture should be soft and sticky. If it isn't, beat the other spare egg white and add a tablespoon at a time until you get the right consistency.

Put the almonds in a bowl – drop a tablespoon of the mixture into the nuts and roll into a ball. Coating the biscuits like this helps to stop them sticking to the baking tray. Place the balls onto the baking tray about 2-3cms apart.

Bake for 18 – 20 minutes or until golden. Allow to cool on a rack and dust with icing sugar.

NOTTAGE POTTAGE

Pottage is a term for a thick soup or stew made by boiling vegetables, grains, and, if available, meat or fish and was a staple food for many centuries. The word pottage comes from the same Old French root as potage, which is a dish of more recent origin.

Pottage consists of various ingredients easily available to serfs and peasants and could be kept over the fire for a period of days, during which time some of it could be eaten, and more ingredients added. The result was a dish that was constantly changing. When wealthier people ate pottage, they would add more expensive ingredients such as meats. The pottage that these people ate was very similar to the Welsh cawl, which is a broth, soup or stew often cooked on and off for days at a time over the fire in a traditional inglenook.

The ancient village of Nottage has 3 excellent pubs all within stumbling distance of one another. I cannot guarantee you will find a bowl of pottage on your visit, but what I can guarantee is fine foods, extensive menu's, a wide range of beers and a warm welcome.

125g carrots, parsnips, onions, and turnips.

1200 ml vegetable stock

125g leeks

125g pearl barley

125g of mushrooms

125g broad beans (or tinned)

125g cabbage

175ml red wine

Salt and Pepper

In a large stew pot, add diced carrots, diced parsnips, diced onion, diced turnips and sweat down using 400ml of the vegetable stock.

After 10-15 minutes, add diced leeks, sliced mushrooms, broad beans (or tinned, rinsed, and drained), and chopped cabbage. Let that simmer for a few minutes and then add 800ml of vegetable stock or as much as you need to cover the veg.

Season with pepper and salt to your taste and add the red wine. Bring the liquid to a boil, and then down to a low heat and cover. Let simmer for 30 minutes. Stir in pearl barley and continue simmering for another 30 minutes, or until cooked.

Add any additional seasoning if desired and serve with a crusty loaf of bread.

Tip: if you want it thicker simmer for longer or try adding a small bit of corn starch that has been mixed with cold water first.

JOLLY SAILOR CREMPOG

This dish is unashamedly named after my local pub The Jolly Sailor. In 1818, the Jolly Sailor became Newton's first licensed premises as a brew house. The establishment instantly became the smugglers headquarters and as the Lords of the Manors had dealings with them by exacting dues on cargos brought from Newton Weir this illegal trade was ignored.

The 'Jolly' is Porthcawl's oldest pub. Facing the green and 12th Century St John the Baptist church. Great beer, great setting, and even better company.

Welsh crempog (also known as Ffroes) differ from the British/French crêpe. They're more like American pancakes and bigger than Scotch pancakes, and often served stacked in a pile and smothered with butter. The stack can be sliced like a wedge of cake and eaten as a teatime treat.

55g butter

450 ml warm buttermilk

275g plain flour

75g castor sugar

1 teaspoon bicarbonate of soda

½ teaspoon salt

1 tablespoon vinegar (can use balsamic as a variation)

2 eggs (well beaten)

Stir the butter into the warmed buttermilk until melted. Gradually pour the milk and butter into the flour, beating well.

Leave the mixture to stand for at least 30 minutes (or a few hours if possible) before stirring in the sugar, bicarbonate of soda, salt, and vinegar.

Add the eggs and beat well until smooth.

Drop the batter, a tablespoon at a time, onto a heated, greased griddle or frying pan, and cook over a moderate heat until golden brown on both sides.

Keep the crempog warm and continue this method until all the batter is used up.

Spread butter on each pancake and eat while warm. The toppings are your choice!

CONEY BEACH ONION CAKES

This is Welsh comfort food at its finest - layers of sliced potatoes and soft onions cooked together until sticky and golden. In South Wales it is called Winwns.

Coney Beach Amusement Park is at the heart of Porthcawl and sits on Sandy Bay, which is one of seven bays at this historical South Wales seaside town. The Parks' own beach is nearly a mile long and a magnet for surfers and bathers alike with lifeguards on duty during the summer months and with donkey rides, bouncy castles, and trampolines ideal as a safe family destination.

It has all the attractions you will ever want from a traditional seaside fair, with arcades, shooting gallery, side shows, dodgems, the Sizzler Twist, and lots more thrill, family, and children's rides. As well as the fair there are cafes, restaurants (where you may be lucky enough to get an onion cake), a bar and nearby function room which can be hired for private events. Entrance to the Park is FREE and opens throughout the summer season.

200g butter (plus extra for the tin)

drizzle of olive oil

one clove crushed garlic

3 large onions (thinly sliced)

1 leek (thinly sliced)

1kg floury potatoes (Maris Piper or Désirée), peeled and thinly sliced (use a mandolin or the fine slicing blade of a food processor)

150g Caerphilly cheese, crumbled (or another sharp, crumbly cheese)

Heat oven to 180°C. In a large pan, heat a knob of the butter with a drizzle of olive oil. Once the butter is warmed, add the garlic, onions, leek, and some seasoning and cook for 15 mins until the onions are soft and sticky, stirring occasionally. Butter a 22cm cake tin or baking dish (alternatively, you can assemble the cake in the pan you are already using if it is ovenproof).

In a separate pan, melt the remaining butter. Toss the sliced potatoes with the melted butter and plenty of salt and pepper.

Arrange the potato slices over the base of the dish in a neat layer. Top with some of the onion mix, sprinkle over a layer of cheese and continue layering, finishing with a final round of potato slices. Press down firmly with your hands to compact the layers and cover with foil. Bake for 50-60 (removing the foil 15 mins before the end of cooking time) so the potatoes are golden brown and tender. Serve cut into slices or straight from the dish.

COW'S CAWL

Cawl is as welsh as it gets. Ingredients tended to vary, but the most common recipes are with lamb or beef and seasonal vegetables. Cawl is recognised as a national dish of Wales.

The dish is also known as 'lobscows' in areas of North Wales. It is related to the Merseyside version called Scouse (enjoyed by Jolly Sailor regular Phil Duckworth) and Lancashire Hotpot enjoyed by a good friend of mine – David Shorrock.

The dish gets its name 'Cow's Cawl' in reference to my nickname of Cow. Due to the volume of food I put away, it has been referred to that I have four stomachs.

1 kg neck or shoulder Welsh lamb, Welsh beef, or ham hock

1 onion and 1 celery stick (roughly chopped)

3 -4 potatoes (peeled and chopped)

3 carrots (peeled and chopped)

1 small swede and 2 parsnips (peeled and chopped)

2 leeks (washed and sliced)

2 garlic cloves (crushed)

250ml welsh beer (see below)

Around 1ltr of vegetable stock (depending on your taste)

salt and black pepper

Place the meat in a large saucepan, cover with water and bring to the boil. Simmer for 2-3 hours over a low heat. Leave to cool and skim off any fat that has risen to the surface. Cut the meat off the bone and return to the vegetable stock then add the potatoes, carrots, swede, parsnips and leeks and simmer until cooked. Add more vegetable stock if required at this point. Season with salt and black pepper. I normally simmer for around 20-30 minutes.

Depending on your preference, you can thicken the cawl if required with a paste made with cornflour and water. I sometimes use a hand blender to make a smoother version.

If you want a great selection of beers try Bang-on-Brewery, who will deliver to your door in the South Wales area.

www.bangonbrewery.beer

Facebook.com/Bang-on Brewery

NANNIE AND NOAHS PASTIES

Whenever our grandson comes to stay, he wants to cook these with Nannie (my wife Nicola).

The pasty is the food most associated with Cornwall, and fortunately my work takes me there on a regular basis and my favourite is Philps in Hayle. It is regarded as the national dish and accounts for 6% of the Cornish food economy.

Whilst travelling in Argentina, and working in Scotland, I was lucky enough to taste their take on the pasty, such as the empanada in Argentina and the bridie in Scotland.

Pastry:

450g plain flour

2tsp baking powder

1tsp salt

125g unsalted butter

2 egg yolks

125ml cold water

Pasty Filling:

450g potato, finely diced

150g onion, finely chopped

300g welsh lamb flank, finely chopped (beef skirt if you want to go Cornish)

Salt and black pepper

1tbsp plain flour

40g butter

1 egg, beaten

100ml welsh ale

To make the pastry, put the salt, butter, flour, baking powder, and egg yolks into a food mixer and mix until the mixture forms crumbs. Slowly add the water until the pastry forms – you may not need all the water. Wrap the pastry in clingfilm and leave it to chill in the fridge for an hour.

To prepare the pasty filling - Preheat the oven to 180°C. Roll out the pastry to the thickness you like. Use a plate as a template and cut out round discs of pastry. I use a big plate but then I am greedy. Use whatever plate suits you. As Noah is 7, we use a smaller plate.

Put the lamb into a bowl and mix with the flour and some salt and pepper. Place some potatoes, onions, and lamb on one half of the circle, leaving a gap round the edge. Dot with butter. Brush around the edge of the pastry circle with the beaten egg, then fold the pastry over the vegetables (season the vegetables separately with salt and black pepper) and meat.

Starting at one side, pinch the edges over to form a sealed semi-circular shaped pasty. Brush the whole pasty with beaten egg, then make a steam hole in the centre with a knife.

Repeat to make the other pasties. Put the pasties in the oven and cook for 50 mins until they are crispy and golden, and the filling is cooked through. Leave them to rest for 5-10 mins before eating.

NORMA'S CURRY

This dish is named after my Mum, Norma who passed away in 2018. She taught me to cook, for which I am forever grateful, on top of many other things that I am grateful to her for. If you take one thing from this book, let it be the opportunity to cook or share an eating experience of these dishes with those close to you - son, daughter, father, mother, grand-children or friends. Life is too short not to.

Life is also too short to slave over a stove, so this version uses short cuts and tinned products.

3 tins of Stewed Steak

2 teaspoons of Lazy Garlic

4 tbsp olive oil

Red and green peppers (finely sliced)

400g tin of chopped tomatoes

Tomato puree

Oxo / Knorr beef stock cube

200g onions (sliced)

½ tin of Pataks Madras paste

Onion powder.

In a large heavy-bottomed saucepan heat the oil on a medium heat. Add the garlic, onions and onion powder and fry for 5-6 minutes until the onions are sweated nicely, remove from heat and place into a food blender. Into the blender also add the tinned tomatoes and blend to a smooth mixture.

Make around 300ml of beef stock.

Place the mixture from the blender back into the saucepan, and add the tinned beef, curry paste, peppers, and squirt of tomato puree.

Bring to a simmer and add the beef stock bit by bit until you get the consistency that you prefer. Once happy with the consistency, simmer for around 20 minutes on a low heat until the meat is cooked.

Note: if you like it hotter or milder, just select the paste you prefer, or add chillies etc. You can also adjust the number of tins of beef to your preferences.

COW CHOW

This dish is a version of Bunny Chow, which is a South African fast food dish consisting of a hollowed-out loaf of white bread filled with curry. The background to this dish is complex and starts from my school days in Lliswerry (yes its 2L's), when me and my friends (Phil Watkins, Andrew Welsh, John Reid and Stuart Marsh) used to go to Graham Howells Bakery on Nash Grove, Newport to buy half a loaf of bread.

We would gouge out and eat the warm dough, and then fill the space left with crisps and eat the rest of the loaf. Ever since then, I have been filled half loaves of bread with all sorts of different foods.

When I visited my family in South Africa, I was introduced to Bunny Chow, and I thought I had died and gone to heaven.

Loaf of Crusty white bread

Norma's Curry (on previous page)

Make Norma's curry as per recipe on previous page.

Warm the bread in the oven / microwave until it's just warm (not too hot).

Cut the bread in half and scoop out the dough. Make sure you do not make any holes in the bread wall as you will need this as a bowl.

Options for the dough are to either eat it warm straight away (is there anything better?) or roll into small dough balls for use later.

Use the hollowed-out bread as a bowl and pour the warm curry into the empty shell crust. If you kept the small dough balls you can drop these into the curry like dumplings, or just dip the warm bread into the curry.

RHYS' HAS A BEEF WITH TRAINING

This for when you come home after a cold winter's night on the rugby training pitch at Ashford RFC.

This dish has an Italian twist due to the influence of my Uncle Franco, who was a Chef is Swansea. He used to cook a version he called Stufato di Manzo. I am mixing up my metric and imperial so apologies for that, but it's what I understand. As I said previously, I don't really measure anything so most of it is via trial and error.

2 tablespoons olive oil
1kg of lean welsh beef (trimmed cut into 1-inch cubes)
2 large onions (chopped)
300g celery (chopped)
4 large carrots (chopped)
200g mushrooms (sliced)
2 tablespoons lazy garlic
glass of red wine
½ tin tomatoes (chopped)
400g potatoes (cut into 1-inch chunks)
1 teaspoon fresh thyme
4 fresh basil leaves (ripped)
½ teaspoon dried sage
600ml beef stock

Heat olive oil in a large pan over medium-high heat. Cook beef in hot oil until browned completely. Remove from pan and put on a plate. Keeping the pan over the heat and retaining the beef drippings. Add the onion, celery, and carrots until just softened, 2 to 3 minutes. Stir mushrooms and garlic.

Pour red wine into the pan and bring to a boil while deglazing the pan with a wooden spoon. Continue cooking the mixture until the wine evaporates - around 8-10 minutes. Stir tomatoes into the mixture. Return the beef to the pan with potatoes, basil, thyme, and sage. Pour beef stock over the mixture. Bring the liquid to a simmer. Reduce heat to low and simmer until the beef is very tender and the sauce is thick, which is about 2 hours. Pop it on low before you go training, and its ready when you get home.

OWAIN'S GYM RECOVERY

This is another nod to my Uncle Franco. Pastina is a type of small pasta added to soups.

Many people consider the most important meal of the day to be breakfast, but for me every meal is important! Current science says that post-workout nutrition may be more important to you than breakfast. In fact, as a rugby coach, I would probably agree that your post-workout meal is one of the most important meals you can have all day.

My favourite machine at the gym is the vending machine.

125g Pastina

1/4 teaspoon salt

1 large egg (lightly beaten)

1 teaspoon butter

1 tablespoon freshly grated Parmesan

Fresh ground black pepper

Bring some water to boil in small saucepan.

Add the Pastina and salt and cook until most of the water is absorbed, this takes around 3-4 minutes or whatever the instructions on your pasta packet suggests.

Turn off heat and stir in egg, letting it cook in the hot pasta. The add the butter, cheese, and pepper.

Depending on your training needs, you could add more eggs, or just use egg whites.

Do you know where Harry Potter keeps his weights at Hogwarts? Behind the dumbbell door.

BETHAN'S BAKES

A strength and conditioning coach is a physical exercise coach whose goal is to improve the performance of individual players or a team – otherwise known as a sadist.

As a Strength and Conditioning Coach, nutrition is always the 'elephant in the room'. However, you cannot be good all the time and hard work requires reward.

250 g Almond Flour

125 g Sugar

3 Whipped Egg Whites

125 g Softened Butter

5 g Vanilla Extract

Large Cadbury's Buttons

In a bowl put egg whites, butter and vanilla then pour sugar and almond flour then stir well.

Place the mixture into a piping bag and make round biscuit shapes on a baking pan with parchment.

Decorate with chocolate buttons and let it stand for 2hours. Use these 2 hours to beast it up and work on your boulders and your biceps, so when you lift these goodies to your mouth you can sell two tickets for the 'gun' show. Just beware the DOMS.

Bake in preheated oven at 180°C for 10 minutes until golden.

ANGHARAD'S CHEESECAKE

My niece is a nut and I tell her – so it had to be Nutella.

Nutritional Information / Calories – In all honesty it is a cheesecake, it is not good for you, so you'd better work this out for yourself. Just enjoy it.

280 g Digestive chocolate biscuits

120 g Butter (unsalted)

600 ml Double cream lightly whipped until it forms soft peaks

400 g cream cheese (full fat)

75 g Icing sugar (sifted)

1 Lemon (juiced)

600 g Nutella

To decorate

150 g Nutella

100 g Roasted chopped almonds / hazelnuts / walnuts (depending on your preference)

Crush the biscuits like you hate them until they look like a cheesecake base.

Mix with the melted butter and press into your cheesecake tin.

Combine the whipped cream, icing sugar, cream cheese, lemon juice. Fold in gently until fully combined. Add the 600g Nutella and stir in thoroughly.

Smooth on top of the biscuit base and flatten the top with the back of a spoon or your boyfriend's credit card.

Put into the freezer for 2 hours.

Gently warm the 150g Nutella (on the hob or microwave for around 15- 20 seconds) and pour over the top. Cover with the chopped nuts of your choice.

Return to the freezer for an hour. After an hour remove the cheesecake from the freezer and remove from the tin.

Leave to stand for about 30 minutes at room temperature before serving with the tears of your enemies.

WOK 'n' ROLL

This is for you buddy. Others know him is Phil, Wocko, Wok (amongst other names) and I have known him for 51 years and am proud to say he is my best mate. We have been through good times and bad and still enjoy each other's company over music, beer and bulls**t.

Both brought up as a single child, we are the brothers each of us never had. Life is partly what we make it, and partly what it is made by the friends we choose.

Mushrooms (large enough to stuff)

Sausage Meat - 2kg

8oz of Cream cheese

Mushroom (finely chopped)

2 cloves Garlic (crushed) / Lazy Garlic

2 tbsp Breadcrumbs

1 tbsp Worcestershire sauce

Parmesan Cheese

Salt & Black Pepper

-

Cook sausage – use any sausage you like but I like Glamorgan Sausages.

Add finely chopped mushrooms, and garlic to sausage and fry for 3-5 minutes.

Turn meat mixture to low heat and add cream cheese, Worcestershire sauce, breadcrumbs, salt, and pepper.

Once cream cheese is fully melted begin to stuff the mushrooms.

Sprinkle extra breadcrumbs and Parmesan cheese over the top.

Bake at 180°C for around 10 minutes.

COW PIE ROLL

I do not really know how to best describe this, so I will not even try. Those of you who know me, will know this is one of my go to treats.

The best way to eat it is obviously after a few beers. Make sure when you eat it, you adopt the correct stance. Feet shoulder width apart and slightly leant over. This avoids the inevitable drip down your shirt or onto your pumps.

Bread roll (buttered)

Peters Mince Pie

Cut the roll open, insert warm pie and eat.

In an emergency, and in the absence of a bread roll, you can substitute bread for a pie sandwich.

THE MORNING AFTER: SIAN'S SALVATION

We have all done it. A wise man once said drinking alcohol is like borrowing fun from tomorrow. This is a good option to help you through the hangover.

Eating, probably feels like the last thing you want to do but is important for getting you on the road to recovery. Some things are better than others for making you feel better.

Depending on how bad you feel, the trusty fry-up is always a great option as it helps replace fatty acids and break down the alcohol in your liver. Eggs are good as they contain something called taurine, which has been shown to reverse the liver damage caused by alcohol.

4 potatoes (thinly sliced)

1 onion (thinly sliced)

4 rashers of smoked bacon (chopped up or use lardons)

2 eggs

Black Pepper

200ml beef stock

Fry the bacon in a thick pan until cooked to your liking. Take the bacon out of the pan but leave the fat and juices in the pan.

Add the onions to the pan and cook them until soft (may need to add a drop of olive oil so they do not stick).

Add the slice of potato and black pepper and mix through. Scatter the back over the top. Add the stock to your liking, but do not let it go any higher than the bacon.

Put a lid on the pan and heavy simmer for around 30 minutes so the potatoes are cooked, and the stock has reduced.

Crack a couple of eggs on top and pop under the grill until cooked.

THE MORNING AFTER: COWS FRY UP

This is another option for the day after redemption. Laverbread is a welsh delicacy from around the Swansea area. It is seaweed that is boiled down into a smooth form and sold in welsh markets. You can also gather it yourself freshly from the beach, and it is also available in canned form. It's the welsh version of Popeye's spinach!

200g Laverbread

Pack of smoked bacon lardons (or diced bacon slices)

200g Cockles

Olive Oil

Eggs

Add the olive oil to a heavy pan and fry the bacon until nice and browned. Add the cockles into the bacon and fry until they are browned.

Add the laverbread to the mixture and fry until very warm. Turn out onto a plate and serve with fired or poached eggs. I serve mine covered in brown sauce, with bread.

THIS PAGE IS INTENTIONALLY LEFT BLANK

Printed by Amazon Italia Logistica S.r.l.
Torrazza Piemonte (TO), Italy